INTRODUCTION

*Lying 90 km ... f Sicily
and 290 km to the n...
1830 km to the ea...
to the west of Alex...
might be said to o...
of the M...*

The group is composed of the islands of Malta, Gozo and Comino all of which are inhabited, and the smaller uninhabited islands of Cominotto, Filfla and St Paul.

The longest distance in Malta in a south-east/north-west axis is about 27 km and the widest distance is 14 km. The corresponding figures for Gozo are 14 km and 7 km. Comino, the smallest of the inhabited islands is 2.6 km². The length of the shoreline around Malta is 136 km and that of Gozo, 43 km. The indentations around the coast form bays, sandy beaches and rocky coves and, more importantly, deep natural harbours.

With a population of around 400,000 crowding an area of 320 km², the Maltese Islands can claim to form the most densely populated country in Europe.

PREHISTORY

Around about 4000 B.C. a group of late Stone Age Sicilian farming families left their island home to settle in a small group of islands to the south. They brought with them their domestic animals, pottery, bags of seeds and flint implements. They were the first Maltese. In time, these early Maltese increased and prospered and, over a considerable period of time, they undertook the construction of temples. Around 1800 B.C. the temple builders disappeared. At one time it was believed that they succumbed to an invasion of fresh migrants

3

The jagged coast around Dwejra on the island of Gozo.

who exterminated, or enslaved, the original settlers and took over the land. The invasion theory cannot be entirely ruled out and still has its adherents. If there was an invasion, the new arrivals, who originally hailed from the heel of Italy, would have had no difficulty in overcoming the remnants of the original stock who had colonized the islands some 2200 years before. If the first settlers were peaceful farmers, the newcomers were more belligerent. These bronze-age pasture farmers were less civilized than the folk they had supplanted. They built no temples but re-used the older, copper-age, temples as cemeteries. The bronze-age farmers were not allowed to enjoy their islands in peace as some 600 years after their arrival a new wave of bronze-using warriors invaded the land, this time in a definite attack for conquest, and made it their home. This event took place around 1200 B.C. Imitating their war-like predecessors, they established their settlements in easily defensible positions. The last of the three ages of antiquity - the Iron Age - is represented in the Maltese Islands by the remains of a single settlement at Baħrija (circa 900 B.C.).

THE PHOENICIANS

The Maltese islands with their fine natural harbours provided an outpost which the Phoenicians founded around 800 B.C. As it was in other countries, so it was in Malta: having gained a foothold as traders, they gradually intermarried and integrated with the bronze-age farmers.

In the case of the Maltese Islands the Phoenicians did venture inland because their artefacts have been found in several places, even as far as Rabat in the centre of the island of Malta. The weaving industry that flourished before the arrival of the Phoenicians probably received an added boost and a wider export market. Pottery was now thrown on a wheel instead of being coiled as was previously the case. The links between the Phoenician colonies and their central state were never very strong and when the Phoenician homeland was overrun it was the colony of Carthage that assumed the role of mother country. In many sectors of the Mediterranean the Phoenicians of Carthage strove to establish a sphere of influence, their chief rivals in this respect being the Greeks. Surprisingly, in the Maltese Islands these differences did not seem to exist: it is not known how many Greeks lived, co-existed rather, with the Phoenicians and the Carthaginians on the island, but some undoubtedly did - civic institutions resembled their Greek counterparts and Greek coins and pottery have been found on the islands.

THE ROMANS

Apparently the Roman invasion did not present great difficulties and it has been suggested that the Phoenicians on the Island turned against their Carthaginian cousins and handed over the garrison to the invading Romans. The Maltese were treated more like allies than as a conquered people: they kept their Punic traditions and language, and their gods. The Romans built the city of Melita, which took the same name as that of the island, over an older, Punic settlement in what is now the Rabat/Mdina area in Malta, as well as another town in Gozo where Victoria (Rabat) now is.

A stone decorated with a spiral motif found at one of Malta's numerous archaeological sites.
Below, aerial view of the island of Comino.

SAINT PAUL

The shipwreck of St Paul in 60 A.D. is recorded in some detail in the Acts of the Apostles, and a Pauline tradition of long standing, supported by archaeological excavations carried out at San Pawl Milqgħi, proves beyond doubt that his arrival in Malta is a historical fact and also that during his three-month stay on the Island he sowed the first seeds of the Christian religion to which

the Maltese people overwhelmingly belong. The Apostle Paul was, at the time, being taken to Rome under arrest to be judged before Caesar as was his right as a Roman Citizen. Amongst the other prisoners was the physician St Luke who recorded the account of that eventful journey. The nearest habitation to the place of shipwreck was the villa of Publius, the chief official of the Island. All those who had been shipwrecked spent three days there and after regaining their strength they moved on to Melita, the main town of the island. In the city Paul cured Publius' father of a fever after which the Roman official converted to Christianity and was later ordained Bishop by St Paul. St. Publius was the first bishop of Malta. After three months, by which time the sea was once more deemed safe for navigation, St Paul sailed to Rome and to his subsequent martyrdom. Tradition has it that a church was built on the site of the palace of Publius, where St Paul had cured his father. Many times rebuilt, the site is now oc-cupied by the Cathedral Church dedicated to St Paul at Mdina.

THE ARABS

The Arab attacks on the islands started around the year 836 during which time Malta and its islands were still under Byzantine rule, but the islands were only conquered in the year 870 by Aglabid Arabs originating from what is now Tunisia, who used Sicily to launch their invasion, as the island had been occupied by them some thirty years previously. To better protect their new territories, the Muslims sectioned off a part of the old Roman town of Melita and defended it with a ditch, calling this citadel Mdina, and the capital of the sister island, Gozo was also divided in the same way; the elite of the small number of Arabs then on the islands probably dwelt in these towns but Arab villages were scattered on both islands. The Arabs introduced the waterwheel, the sienja, an animal-driven device for raising water, now practically obsolete, and, much

The megalithic complex of Ħaġar Qim.

more importantly, the cultivation of the cotton plant, the mainstay of the Maltese economy for several centuries.

THE MIDDLE AGES

The Arabs in Sicily were divided, and taking advantage of the situation, Count Roger the Norman, after a series of campaigns, brought the island under Norman Rule. Count Roger had invaded the islands to make sure his southern flank was secure from a possible Arab attack. In the same year (1090) Count Roger also occupied the Maltese Islands. Having reduced the Arabs to a state of vassalage and released the foreign Christian slaves, he returned to Sicily without even bothering to garrison his prize. In Malta the Normans followed the same enlightened policy and although the Christian faith was regarded as the official religion there, nobody was persecuted for their race or religious beliefs.

Pinto's clock in the Grand Master's Palace, Valletta.

In 1127 Roger II, the son of Count Roger, led a second invasion of Malta; having overrun the island he placed it under the charge of a Norman governor and also garrisoned the three castles then on the islands with Norman soldiers. The last Norman king died without a male heir however, and the new masters of the Maltese islands came, in turn, from the ruling

houses of Germany, France and Spain: the Swabians (1194); the Angevins (1268); the Aragonese (1283) and finally, the Castilians (1410). When the Norman Period came to an end, the Fief of Malta was granted to loyal servants of the Sicilian Crown; these Counts, or Marquises of Malta as these nobles were styled, looked on the fief simply as an investment - a source for the collection of taxes and something to be bartered or sold when no longer viable. The last feudal lord of Malta, Don Gonsalvo Monroy, was expelled from the island following a revolt. By this time, the Maltese were thoroughly Christianized and the houses of the great Religious Orders were being established in the Island: the Franciscans (1370); the Carmelites (1418); the Augustinians (1450); the Dominicans (1466); and the Minor Observants (1492), while the Benedictine Sisters arrived in 1418.

THE KNIGHTS OF THE ORDER OF ST JOHN

As a military order, the Knights took part in the Crusades, but when Acre fell in 1291, they were driven off from their last stronghold in the Holy Land.

After a short stay in Cyprus, the Knights, with the assistance of the Genoese, occupied Rhodes. This was to be their home for the next two hundred years until they were forced to leave the island by the Sultan Suleiman.

After wandering for seven years, the Knights and the refugees from Rhodes who had attached themselves to them, were offered the Island of Malta as a home by the Holy Roman Emperor, Charles V. To the relief of the Maltese Nobles, the Knights decided that Mdina, the capital city, was too far inland and they set about establishing themselves in the small village that had grown up behind the old Castell'a Mare.

In Birgu the Knights organized themselves along the lines they had evolved during their stay in Rhodes. The Order could be described as a multi-national force divided into Langues according to the nationality of its members. These langues, or tongues, were: Auvergne, Provence, France, Aragon, Castile, England, Ger-

Map of Malta published by Quintinus in 1533. Wignacourt Museum, Rabat.

"Final attack of the Turks on Fort St Elmo" by Matteo Perez D'Aleccio. President's Palace, Valletta.

many and Italy. Each langue had its own Auberge, or headquarters, as well as a specific duty traditionally assigned to it, and each langue was also responsible for the defence of a particular post, such as a section of a bastion or tower. As if to prove the inadequacy of the defences of the islands, in 1547, and again in 1551, the Turks launched two attacks against them, the latter being particularly calamitous. Ravaging the Maltese countryside and ignoring the fortified towns, the Turks then turned their attention to the island of Gozo and carried away the entire population into slavery. These attacks pushed the Knights into feverish activity to improve the islands' defences in anticipation of another, and possibly bigger, attack.

THE GREAT SIEGE

"Nothing is better known than the siege of Malta" wrote Voltaire two hundred years after the event and for the Maltese people today the statement still rings true.

The bare bones of the narrative are as follows: On the 18th May 1565, the Ottoman Turks and their allies pitted 48,000 of their best troops against the islands with the intention of invading them, and afterwards to make a thrust into Southern Europe by way of Sicily and Italy.

Against them some 8,000 men were drawn up: 540 Knights; 4000 Maltese; and the rest made up of Spanish and Italian mercenaries. Landing unopposed, the first objective of the Turks was to secure a safe anchorage for their large fleet, and with that in mind, they launched their attack on St. Elmo. After a heroic resistance of thirty-one days the fort succumbed to the massive bombardment and continuous attacks of the Turks. After the fort had been seized, the Ottomans turned their attention to the two badly fortified towns overlooking the harbour, Birgu and Senglea. Subjected to a ceaseless bombardment, and repulsing attack after attack behind the crumbling walls, against all odds the Christian forces kept the enemy at bay until a small relief force of some 8,000 troops arrived from Sicily. The Maltese people were able to drive back the Turks and so to save themselves.

THE FOUNDATION OF VALLETTA

The idea of fortifying the rocky and steep-sided Mount Sciberras had occurred to the Knights on their arrival in 1530, but because time was not on their side, they limited themselves to building a fort at its furthest tip instead.

If other Grand Masters studied the possibilities of such a project, La Valette was obsessed with the idea. As soon as he had been elected Grand Master in 1557 he invited foreign military engineers to prepare the plans, but the Great Siege put a stop to that. No sooner was the siege lifted than the plans for the fortress city were again revived, but as a first step the ill-fated Fort St Elmo was at once rebuilt. Pope Pius IV sent his military engineer, Francesco Laparelli, and the planning of the new town started in earnest. When Laparelli departed from the Island he left his Maltese assistant, Gerolamo Cassar, to continue the work he had started. La Valette died in 1568 and was buried in the Church of Our Lady of Victories, the first building to be erected.

THE FALL OF THE ORDER

When the Order made Malta its home, for the first time the rulers of the Maltese lived on the Island itself, and wealth was brought to the Island, rather than extracted from it. The finances of the Order were now in a precarious situation. Unemployment was rife and poverty was widespread. Towards the end of the 18th century matters

for the Order were going from bad to worse: in France, where most of her overseas property lay, the possessions of the Order were taken over by the Republican Government and French refugees, fleeing to Malta from the Revolution, were an added drain on the treasury of the Order. At the time the last Grand Master of Malta, Ferdinand von Hompesch, was being elected, Napoleon was making his plans to take over the island.

THE FRENCH

Napoleon's capture of Malta in June 1798 cannot be counted as one of his military triumphs.

The Grand Master capitulated without offering any resistance and Napoleon made his grand entry into Valletta while within a week Von Hompesch, accompanied by a few knights, left the Island. The Maltese felt that they had been let down by the Order, but before they could attempt any resistance they were talked into submission by the Bishop. Maltese that had served in the Order's army and navy were recruited into the French Republican forces, and other regiments were raised for garrison duties on the island itself. After stripping the palaces, Auberges and other buildings of everything of value, Napoleon, conveniently forgetting his promises, next turned his attention to the churches; only such articles that were indispensable for the "exercise of the cult" were left while all other valuables were removed and priceless works of art in gold and silver were melted down into ingots. Nominally the Order had held the Island of Malta in fief from the King of Sicily (since 1735 Sicily had been amalgamated with the State of Naples and was then known as the King-

"Portrait of a Maltese courtesan in the 16th century" by Nicola de Nicolay. National Library, Valletta.

THE BRITISH

Once the French were expelled from the Island, the British were not so much interested in possessing Malta, as keeping the French out. In fact, with the Treaty of Amiens (1802) that brought hostilities between Britain and France to an end, it was decided that Malta should be returned to a reformed Order of St John under the protection of the Kingdom of the Two Sicilies and that her neutrality would be guaranteed by all the Great Powers.

With the British in command of the sea, all mercantile shipping was obliged to call at the harbour of Valletta and before long, the Maltese Islands became the most important centre of trade in the Mediterranean. Under the Treaty of Paris (1814) the island was confirmed as a British possession. Agriculture was encouraged to make the Island Fortress as self-sufficient as possible and potato cultivation, now a major agricultural export, was introduced. The

dom of the Two Sicilies), and it was to the King of the Two Sicilies that the Maltese now turned for aid and protection. At the same time deputies were despatched to seek aid from the allies of the King, the British. A small number of British troops were landed and the French in Gozo surrendered in October 1798, the Sicilian flag being hoist on the ramparts. As the siege wore on, the French who were penned in the fortifications, were prevented from receiving aid due to the British blockade, though the Maltese, by this time aided by Italian and British troops, did not have the means to assault the formidable bastions. The French, by now exhausted, were ready to capitulate but Napoleon's troops proudly refused to submit to the Maltese rebels. The British, on the other hand, anxious to deploy their troops and warships in other theatres of war, were eager to speed up the surrender of the French in Malta, which took place in 1800.

THE MALTESE CROSS

This symbol of Malta par excellence was also the symbol of the Order of the Knights of Saint John. The Cross originated in Amalfi; each of its eight points represents one of the heavenly virtues (truth, faith, repentance, humility, justice, mercy, purity, and endurance of persecution) and the eight Langues of the original Knights.

ever present problem of the water supply also received urgent attention. Prosperity brought about a rapid rise in the population and emigration was actively encouraged to ease the burden on the Fortress economy. Italian political refugees of the Risorgimento sought refuge in Malta and the example of these Italian patriots had the effect of further fanning the flames of Maltese nationalism. At the insistence of the Maltese population, a Council of Government was set up in 1835.

The military worth of Malta and its islands was to be demonstrated during the Crimean War (1854-56) when the Island Fortress became a rear base for the departure of troops and a receiving station for casualties.

Imperial policy dictated that Britain take Malta under full protection and anglicize, as far as possible, the local population. The First World War placed Malta on a war footing and, as had happened in the Crimean War sixty years earlier, Malta was to provide harbour and dockyard facilities to the Allied Navies, while her contribution in the cause of sick and wounded soldiers hospitalized on the island earned Malta the title "Nurse of the Mediterranean".

A National Assembly was set up to make proposals for a new constitution. During one of the public meetings of this Assembly, held on the 7th June 1919, the crowd grew hostile and troops were called out to restore order. With the new Constitution approved in 1921, Malta was, at last, to be granted self government with responsibility for all internal affairs. The British Government retained control over Defence, Foreign Affairs, and Immigration.

THE PATH TO INDEPENDENCE

For the Maltese people the path to independence was neither smooth nor straight. By the time Malta was granted self govern-

"The Naval Battle of 3 May 1706: the Knights capture enemy ships." Maritime Museum, Birgu. Right, a detail.

ment in 1921, the political factions could be classified into three main groups: the pro-British group that broadly opted for the advancement of the English language and culture, as well as the dissemination of the Maltese language. The pro-Italian group stood for the use of Italian and English but also for the propagation of Italian culture. The newcomer to the political scene was the Labour Party, then in its infancy, its programme being compulsory education, the promotion of the English and Maltese languages and, as is to be expected, the improvement of working and social conditions. In the troubles that followed, elections were suspended and in 1930 the Constitution was withdrawn. In the subsequent election the pro-Italian party, with the support of the Church, won at the polls with a great majority. In the political storm that followed, the Constitution was again suspended and one year later Malta reverted to colonial rule. The British Government, now in sole control of the island and unfettered by local political opinion, made Maltese and English the two official languages of the Island, which, in fact, they still are, while the use of Italian was eliminated from administrative circles. By the time the next constitution was granted, World War II was under way. When Italy allied herself to Germany, Malta was thrown into the front line. The first attack, by Italian bombers, took place on 11th June 1940. War in the Mediterranean theatre was predictable, yet when it did come the island was poorly equipped to defend itself: the only fighter planes were four antiquated Gloucester Gladiators. These planes were augmented with a few Hurricanes some weeks later. Against these, the Italian Regia Aeronautica could count on two hundred aircraft stationed in Sicily, a mere hundred kilometres from Malta. In June 1941 Hitler attacked Russia and the Luft-

Maltese costumes of the 16th and 17th centuries. National Library, Valletta.

waffe in Sicily diverted most of its planes to that front. The air-raids on Malta eased, but did not cease entirely; at the same time, having received reinforcements, Malta took to the offensive and submarines and aircraft based on the Island attacked Axis shipping as well as ground targets in Sardinia, Sicily and even Tripoli; furthermore, by intercepting supplies from Sicily to North Africa, Rommel was deprived of many essential supplies. On 26th July 1941 the only seaborne attack, directed against the Grand Harbour by Italian E-boats, was brave and dashing, but unsuccessful. When the Luftwaffe returned to Sicily in full complement, the bombing commenced once more and Malta was again thrown on the defensive. A third of the anti-aircraft crews were Maltese and they soon made a name for themselves with their bravery and efficiency. On 15th April 1942 King George VI awarded the George Cross Medal to "... the brave people of the Island Fortress of Malta". If the morale of Malta's defenders was high, the

material resources of the Island were low; with supply ships being intercepted and destroyed by Axis aircraft and submarines the situation was desperate. By July 1942 the supply of vital provisions was calculated to last two weeks. Although badly mauled, the "Santa Maria Convoy" limped into the Grand Harbour on 15th August of that year and the situation was saved. With replenished stores and the arrival of some hundred Spitfires, the tables, at last, were being turned. In July 1943, using Malta as an advance base, the Allies invaded Sicily and the war moved away from the island. True to their promise made during the War, the British restored self government. Fresh elections were held and the pro-Italian exiles were repatriated. As most of the inhabitants were homeless, reconstruction was the first priority of the newly elected Labour Government, but social conditions were also improved. In the area around the docks especially, the trade union movement grew in strength as workers everywhere were becoming conscious of their rights. Three years later, following a split in the Labour Party, the Nationalist Party headed a Coalition Government and this party now strove to obtain Dominion status for the island. Originally the party representing the intelligentsia, it now attracted numerous workers within its ranks. On the return of the Labour Party to office, a request for integration was made to the British Government with Maltese representation at Westminster. When the British began to appear reluctant, after evincing an initial interest, the Labour Party went to the other extreme and insisted on Independence; the acrimonies that followed were to cost the Labour Party many votes. The Constitutional Party, the original pro-British party, died a natural death, its mission having been accomplished. In the wake of fresh elections and confirmed by a referendum, Malta achieved Independence within the Commonwealth on 21st September 1964 with the Queen of England as the nominal Queen of Malta. Under the next Labour Government, Malta was declared a Republic with Sir Anthony Mamo as its first President. On 31st March 1979, on termination of the Military Base Agreement, the last British serviceman left the island and Malta entered into a self-imposed state of neutrality. Tourism remains one of the key pillars of Malta's earnings although local manufacturing, largely with foreign investors, also plays an important role in the Maltese economy. The Maltese are a proud and independent people but they are realistically aware that financially Malta cannot stand alone. Since 1 May 2004 Malta has been a member of the European Union.

Grand Master's Palace, late 19th century, as seen by K. F. Brockdorf. National Library, Valletta.

The tourist harbour of Vittoriosa with the church of St Lawrence in the background.

GOZO

COMI

St Barbara ramparts, Valletta.

MALTA

Malta is the main, and the largest, island of the Maltese archipelago. The capital of the Republic of Malta, Valletta, is located here as well as other important cities such as Mdina, the old capital, and Rabat. The island is densely packed with buildings, especially in the area around Valletta, and often it is difficult to know where the boundaries between the various cities and towns lie.

But despite this each has its own characteristics.

There are interesting archaeological sites on Malta providing evidence of ancient, highly-developed civilizations that dwelt here in prehistoric times, in addition to the important monuments, churches and fortifications built by the Knights of the Order of St John, present on the island for about three centuries. Malta is also noted for its connection with St Paul who lived here for three months following a shipwreck during his voyage to Rome.

Malta is rather flat (the highest point reaches only 258 metres) and the terrain consists of limestone and clay. The coastline is high and rocky to the south west while to the east there are numerous bays and inlets such as Marsaxlokk and the Grand Harbour. To the north instead, there are sandy beaches where one can spend relaxing days by the sea. Lastly, various places in the area around Valletta provide entertainment for lovers of nightlife, the best known of which is St Julian's.

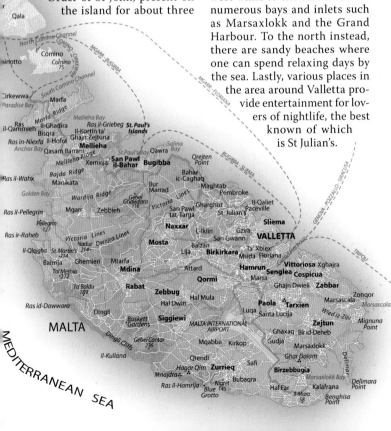

Above, view of Valletta from the harbour
of Marsamxett.

Below, aerial view of the city built
on the Sciberras peninsula.

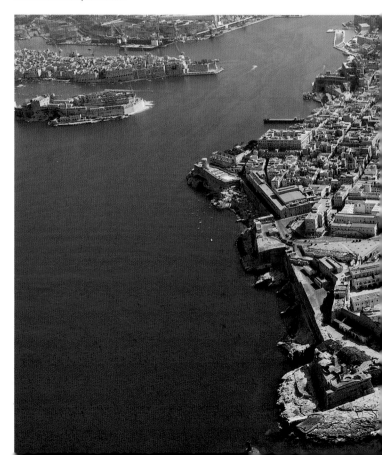

VALLETTA

When Grand Master Jean Parisot de la Valette laid the foundation stone of Humilissima Civitas Vallettae, the last thing that he had in mind was a city of fine palaces. Valletta was intended as a fortress to protect the two harbours on either side of the rocky peninsula on which it was to be built.

The first buildings to be erected were the Auberges: these were the headquarters of the different ethnic groups into which the Knights were divided. The **National Library**, the Biblioteca, was the last building to have been built by the Order, having been finished in 1796. It houses a rich collection of books as well as medieval manuscripts and the archives of the Order. As a memento one can buy a photocopy of the deed of Emperor Charles V in which he granted Malta and its islands in fief to the Order in 1530.

Even if the Opera House has yet to rise from the ashes of the Blitz (some are of the opinion that a multi-storey car park should be built there instead), music lovers

and balletomanes can still go to **Manoel Theatre**. This gem of a building was built in 1732 and has recently been restored to its former glory for, as its builder Grand Master Anton Manoel de Vilhena would have said, "... the honest recreation of the people". For art lovers there are the **Museum of Fine Arts** and the **Cathedral Museum**. Valletta boasts three parish churches (two of these are the *Church of St Paul's Shipwreck* and *Our Lady of Victories*) and a host of others,

but pride of place must go to **St John's Co-Cathedral**. The plain exterior of this edifice grossly belies its sumptuous interior: no space is left unadorned, the walls are carved and gilded and the painted vaulted ceiling is a masterpiece by Mattia Preti, while four hundred slabs of inlaid marble pave the church. These slabs are emblazoned with the armo-rial bearings of the more important members of the Order. In years gone by, people, especially young people, used to troop into Valletta every evening, filling the many cinemas, crowding the coffee shops, or just strolling up and down the main streets to see and be seen, followed by a last-minute rush to catch the last bus to the village.

Opposite page, above, a section of the ramparts that surround Valletta.

Centre left, the Café Premier Complex in Republic Square; right, a street in Valletta.

Right, the Malta Siege Bell, made in memory of the 7000 victims of the Second World War.

Below, busy City Gate Square.

THE GRAND MASTERS' PALACE

Valletta is a city of palaces but for the Maltese, the Grand Masters' Palace is known simply as *il Palazz*, the Palace.

In its finished form the Palace is built on two floors and occupies an entire block. The two main portals, Baroque and imposing, stand in direct contrast to the unadorned treatment of the rest of the façade; three other side entrances give on to as many streets. Three of the doorways lead to a spacious courtyard while another portal and a gate lead to a smaller courtyard on a

slightly higher level. The larger of the two courtyards is known as the **Neptune Courtyard** after the bronze statue of the god there. The smaller courtyard - the **Prince Alfred Courtyard** - is named after one of Queen Victoria's sons to commemorate his visit to Malta in 1858, but this courtyard is better known as that of **Pinto's Clock**. This clock has four dials showing - besides the time - the day, the month and the phases of the moon. The hours are struck by bronze effigies of Moorish slaves wielding sledge-hammers. It is said to be the work of the Maltese clockmaker Gaetano Vella and was made in 1745.

As in Renaissance palaces in Italy, the most important floor was the first, the Piano Nobile, the ground floor being used as stables, service quarters and stores. The *Main Staircase* leading up to the Piano Nobile was built by Grand Master Hughes de Loubenx Verdala identified by the wolf in the coat of arms. The top of the staircase gives on to a lobby formed by the angle where two of the palace corridors meet. The right-hand passage leads to what used to be the Palace **Armoury** but that part of the building is now the seat of the House of Representatives. The *lunettes* over the windows in this passage are the work of Nicolò Nasoni da Siena and were painted in the first quarter of the 18th century. The corresponding works were painted by the Maltese artist Giovanni Bonello some hundred and sixty years later; together, however, the two series are complementary and show Maltese and Gozitan landscapes as they appeared at those times.

The **Council,** or **Tapestry, Chamber** in the Armoury Cor-

Statue of Neptune in the Neptune Courtyard.
Opposite page, above, a carriage in front of the Grand Master's Palace.
Below, the external gallery of the Palace.

ridor is an impressive hall where the members of the Order sat in Council. On being elected to office, a Grand Master was expected to make a gift to the Order - the Gioja. Part of the Gioja of Grand Master Ramon Perellos y Rocaful is the priceless set of **Gobelins Tapestries** that give the name to this chamber. Perellos was elected in 1697 but it was only in 1710 that these tapestries were completed and hung in the place for which they had been created. *Les Tentures des Indes* (the Indian Tapestries) is a rather vague title for the magnificent rendering of fauna and flora from three continents, the Noble

Savage also being very much in evidence.

To the left of the lobby at the top of the Main Staircase is another corridor, known as the **Entrance Corridor**. This too, like the Armoury Corridor, is decorated with *paintings* by Nicolò Nasoni, but this time the subject chosen for the decoration of the lunettes are scenes of naval battles between the Order's galleys and those of the Ottoman Turks, apparently a subject dear to the hearts of these seafaring Knights.

The first door to the right of the lobby leads into the **State Dining Room**. Here the British con-

Above, entrance to the Neptune Courtyard.
Left, decoration above the door into the Chamber of Representatives.

nection is well represented by several *Royal portraits*. The next door along the Entrance Corridor leads to the **Hall of the Supreme Council**, also known as the **Throne Room**. Like all the other ceilings of the Piano Nobile, the wooden ceiling of this hall is elaborately coffered and painted, but the item of greatest interest here is a *frieze of twelve frescoes* by Matteo Perez d'Aleccio who worked in Malta between 1576 and 1581.

Against the far end of the wall is the *throne*, occupied first by

The main entrance to the upper floor with the coat of arms of the Republic of Malta in the foreground.

the Grand Masters and then by the British Governors. Above the throne are now the arms of the Republic of Malta.

Across the hall and opposite the throne a carved **minstrels' gallery** is set into the wall; this carved and painted gallery is said to have been part of the Order's flagship, the Great Carrack of Rhodes, one of the vessels that carried the Knights to Malta. A door from the Throne Room leads to the **Ambassadors' Room**, also known as the **Red Room** from the colour of its damask hanging.

In one of the panels, Knights of

Council Chamber, also known as the Tapestry Chamber: detail of the tapestries of the Indies, by Gobelin.

the Order are shown holding shields bearing the white eight-pointed (or Maltese) cross on a red background; this could be poetic licence on the part of the painter because the battle standard of the Order was a plain white cross on a red background, not unlike the Danish Flag. A door from the Ambassadors' Room leads to the **Paggeria**, the Pages' Waiting Room, also known as the **Yellow Room** after the gold damask covering of its walls.

A door from the Pages' Waiting Room leads into a corridor which is at a right angle to the Entrance Corridor. This is known as the **Prince of Wales Corridor** in commemoration of a visit by King Edward VII, then Prince of Wales, in 1862.

The rooms along this passage were formerly the **private apartment of the Grand Master**; later they were used as the offices of the British Governors. These rooms are now the offices of the President of the Republic.

The *private chapel* of the Grand Master was turned into an office for the use of the Governor's Secretary and the minstrels' gallery, now in the Throne Room, was originally here. The *paintings* in this chapel are probably the earliest found in the palace and show *episodes from the life of St John the Baptist*, the patron saint of the Order.

ARMOURY MUSEUM

As presently displayed, the collection is small but interesting. On the death of a Knight his armoury becomes the property of the Order.

The collection today contains over 5000 items dating from the 16th to the 18th century including the *armoury of Alof de Wignacourt* and of *Valette*, two of the most important Grand Masters of the Order.

At the time of the arrival of the Order in Malta, in 1530, the use of firearms was rapidly revolutionizing warfare - the Great Siege was fought largely with artillery and arquebuses but armour still had its uses - a century later breastplates and shields were still being tested against firearms, and in the Armoury there are several examples with dents in them to prove that they were "bullet-proof".

Knights' armoury displayed in the museum.
A room in the Armoury Museum.

27

ST JOHN'S CO-CATHEDRAL

In 1573 Grand Master Jean de la Cassière authorized the construction of a conventual church of the Order of St John. It was completed in 1578 by the Maltese architect Gerolamo Cassar. Its austere exterior gives no indication of the opulent and extravagant interior. A modest *portico* over the main door supports the balcony used by the Grand Master to present himself to the public after election. The rectangular baroque **interior** was embellished by successive Grand Masters and further enriched by the "Gioja" or gift, which every Knight was bound by statute to give on admission to the Order. Between 1662-1667, Mattia Preti "Il Calabrese" painted the *Life of St John the Baptist*, patron saint of the Order, directly on to the primed stone of the ceiling. The Cottoner brothers paid for this work. The *altar* is made of Lapis lazuli and other rare marbles. The Episcopal throne was originally reserved for the Grand Master. The side chapels were allotted to each of the "Langues" of the Order

Above, detail of the Co-Cathedral.

Left, one of the bell towers and a chapel near the Co-Cathedral.

and the Grand Masters belonging to each particular langue are buried here. The gates in the **Chapel of the Holy Sacraments**, like the candlesticks on the main altar, are made of silver. The Grand Masters who died at Malta before the church was completed are buried in the **Crypt**, the most important sarcophagi being

The façade of St John's Co-Cathedral, designed by the Maltese architect, Gerolamo Cassar.

Right, the baroque interior of the Co-Cathedral: the high altar.

those of La Valette, victor of the Great Siege of 1565 and La Cassière who built St John's. In the ornate *Oratory* is a 3 by 5 metre painting by Caravaggio depicting the **Beheading of St John**. This painting is regarded as Caravaggio's greatest masterpiece and is the only one of his paintings which bears his signature.

The splendid organ in St John's
Co-Cathedral.
Left, another detail
of the cathedral interior.

Opposite page, above, a room
in the Museum of St John's
Co-Cathedral.

Centre left, one of the works
in the Museum; right, St John's
Co-Cathedral in a 17th-century
painting. Museum of Fine Arts,
Valletta.

Below, general view of the cathedral
interior showing the vaults frescoed
by Mattia Preti and illustrating 18
episodes from the "Life of St John
the Baptist".

The "Beheading of St John the Baptist" by Caravaggio, 1608.

Above, "St Jerome" by Caravaggio, 1608. Museum of St John's Co-Cathedral.

Left, view of the oratorio showing Caravaggio's painting of the "Beheading of St John the Baptist".

CARAVAGGIO IN MALTA

Caravaggio fled to Malta when he was threatened with imprisonment for a murder. Here, in 1608, commissioned by the Grand Master Alof de Wignacourt, he painted the "Beheading of St John the Baptist" to adorn the altar dedicated to the saint. The scene takes place in a prison as is evident from the faces of two prisoners watching from behind a grating. The body of the saint most probably represents that of the murder victim. Caravaggio has placed his signature in the blood flowing from his neck. In Malta Caravaggio was granted the title of "Knight of Grace" by the Order on 14 July 1608. On 6 December, however, he was expelled following a row (and subsequent arrest) with a Knight of a higher rank.

REPUBLIC STREET AND MERCHANTS STREET

These two parallel streets represent the main thoroughfares of the city. From early morning both are extremely busy. **Republic Street** is longer, higher and broader and has many bars, cafes and shops. The *churches of St Barbara* and *St Francis* are located here. In **Merchants Street** there is a little market where all kinds of items are sold, as well as many goldsmiths' studios and jewellers' shops.

Top, daily market in Merchants Street.

Left, typical Maltese "karrozin".

Bottom left, busy Republic Street.

Below, the food market.

*The Salon in Admiralty House, where
the National Museum of Fine Arts is located.*

NATIONAL MUSEUM OF FINE ARTS

South Street is one of the most elegant streets in the city. It was originally known as Strada del Palazzo after the Magistrates Palace which was to be built here. This street was also known as Strada d'Albergo di Francia after the Auberge de France, destroyed during the last war, situated in it.

Admiralty House with the **National Museum of Fine Arts** is one of the palaces gracing this street. This was one of the first buildings erected in Valletta, but it was rebuilt in its present form between 1761 and 1765. During the French occupation it was offered to the Bishop of Malta to be used as a seminary. On the capitulation of the French garrison, "Casa Miasi" as the palace then became known, was occupied by the Commander of the Anglo-Maltese troops, Captain Alexander Ball.

In 1808, Louis Charles Viscount de Beaujolais, and his brother Louis Philippe, Duke of Orléans arrived and were lodged in this palace; it was here that the Viscount de Beaujolais died. The premises were leased to the British naval authorities in 1821 and the palace remained the official residence of the Commander-in-Chief of the British Mediterranean Fleet. In 1961 it was handed over to the Maltese Government and in 1974 it was restored to its former glory and converted into a Museum of Fine Arts. It houses *paintings, sculpture, furniture* and *objects* connected with the Order of St John. Permanently displayed in this Museum are works by Reni, Valentini, Stomer, Preti, Tiepolo, Favray and Perugino. A section is specially reserved for works by Maltese artists. Temporary exhibitions and lectures are also held here.

AUBERGE DE PROVENCE
AND THE NATIONAL MUSEUM OF ARCHAEOLOGY

The **Auberge de Provence** was built between 1571 and 1575 to a design by the Maltese architect Gerolamo Cassar. The façade was altered during the first half of the 18th century. The Auberge was the residence of the Langue de Provence, its Head, the "Grand Commandeur" being the Treasurer of the Order. From 1820 to 1954 the building housed the British officers' Union Club; it is now the **National Museum of Archaeology**. The Auberge contains a valuable *collection of prehistoric artefacts* such as pottery, statuettes, stone implements, personal and other ornaments recovered from Malta's prehistoric and megalithic temple sites. Several table *models* of these temples are on permanent display and tomb furniture from the Punic and Roman periods is also exhibited.

*Above, the "Venus of Malta".
Right, the "Sleeping Woman",
discovered in the Ħal Saflieni
Hypogeum in Paola.
Below, a room in the
National Archaeological
Museum.*

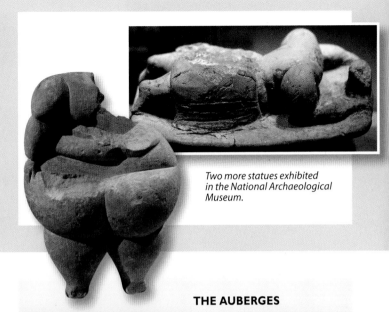

Two more statues exhibited in the National Archaeological Museum.

The impressive façade of the Auberge de Provence.

THE AUBERGES

The Order of the Knights of St. John was divided into "Langues" (nationalities), each of which maintained an "Auberge": a residence with a chapel, refectories, and other rooms set out around a courtyard. The auberges were originally eight in number and were all built in Vittoria. When the new city of Valletta came into being, the Auberges were built here too, though they were reduced to seven as Henry VIII suppressed the English order following his dispute with the Pope. The English knights thus had no headquarters exclusively of their own in the new city. The Auberges were all built by Gerolamo Cassar between 1571 and 1590. Today only five still remain: the **Auberge d'Italie** in Merchants Street which now also houses the Malta Tourism Authority, the **Auberge de Provence** in Republic Street, the **Auberge d'Aragon**, the oldest and simplest structure, the **Auberge d'Angleterre e Bavière** and the **Auberge de Castille**.

AUBERGE DE CASTILLE

The **Auberge de Castille, Leon and Portugal**, is the largest and perhaps finest of all the Auberges. Its head was the Grand Chancellor of the Order of St John.

It was first built in 1574 by Gerolamo Cassar on a site originally earmarked for the Magistrates Palace. Extensive reconstructions were undertaken in 1744 during Grand Master Pinto de Fonseca's term of office. Domenico Cachia, the architect responsible for these modifications, was influenced by the Prefettura at Lecce and produced a very imposing façade.

*Top, the elegant façade
of the Auberge de Castille,
now the Prime Minister's offices.
Above, the monumental entrance.*

The monument dedicated to Alexander Ball in Lower Barracca Gardens. Below, the colonnade in Upper Barracca Gardens.

BARRACCA GARDENS

The Gardens, once private, are now open to the public. A fabulous view across the Grand Harbour and the Three Cities can be enjoyed from both the **Upper** and **Lower Barracca Gardens**. The Upper Barracca Gardens were created in 1661 by the Italian Knight, Flaminio Barbiani. The Gardens are enhanced by numerous statues including the group of *Les Gavroches* by the Maltese artist Antonio Sciortino and a *colonnade* of the 16th century. There is a delightful little *temple* in the Lower Barracca Gardens, dedicted to Alexander Ball who lead the Maltese against the French.

FORT ST ELMO

The Fort was built by the Knights in 1551 and was originally star-shaped. In 1565 during the great siege, the Fort fell to the Turks after 31 days. After the defeat of the Turks, the Fort was given its present appearance by Laparelli. Later, further changes were made but these concerned the position of the weaponry, rather than the structure.

The entrance to Fort St Elmo.

Opposite page, two views of the Fort.

NATIONAL WAR MUSEUM

Housed inside the Fort is the **National War Museum** where the *cross* given to Malta by King George VI during the Second World War and the *Gloucester Gladiator*, one of the three airplanes active in the region at the beginning of the conflict, are exhibited.

Above, a room in the National War Museum in Fort St Elmo.

Left, the Gloucester Gladiator, one of the airplanes exhibited in the Museum.

CARNIVAL

One of the best periods of the year to visit Malta is Carnival time. The festivities reach their most frenetic at Valletta, but fascinating events are also held in the small towns of the other islands, and in particular at Nadur on Gozo. During Carnival, thousands of brightly-dressed revelers invade the city streets to

watch the parades with their fantastical floats. In Paceville you can party all night moving from one club to another. And this week is undoubtedly the very best for making one's acquaintance with the vitality and festive spirit of the Maltese.

TOUR OF THE GRAND HARBOUR

The Grand Harbour is situated on an inlet 4 kilometres long. Boat trips around the port are available, and also provide an introduction to the history of the island. The Grand Harbour is guarded by Fort St Elmo (where the damage caused by Italian forces in 1941 is still visible) and the Ricasoli Fort. From the tour boats, the ramparts and the Upper and Lower Barracca Gardens of Valletta can be seen. To the east, opposite the capital city, are Vittoriosa and Senglea, separated by the Cottonera Lines, a 2-kilometre long wall built for defensive purposes in 1670. The entire area is overlooked by Fort St Angelo at Vittoriosa.

SLIEMA AND ST. JULIAN'S

*Sliema and St Julian's are the main centres of tourism
in Malta. Both towns provide all kinds of entertainment
in the numerous hotels, restaurants, shops,
bars and clubs.*

*Warm winter sun on the Sliema seafront.
Below, Independence Gardens in Sliema.*

Around the 1850s **Sliema** became a summer resort for the well-to-do and, before long, the resort grew into a town. The rich built their villas on the ridge, away from the rougher area where the fisher folk lived. As the British servicemen left, the tourists moved in, and the houses of Sliema - both the villas and the hovels - were pulled down and blocks of flats and hotels appeared in their stead. A fort built by the British in 1872 is now an excellent pizzeria. The promenade is probably the most densely populated area in the Island as strollers enjoy the sea-breezes in the cool of the

The church of Sliema and part of the beach in this attractive town. Below, view of St Julian's and the harbour.

summer evenings. **St Julian's**, its suburb, can claim an older ancestry. Originally this hamlet sprang up around the old chapel dedicated to Saint Julian, patron of hunting (first built in 1580, but many times rebuilt). The *hunting lodges* of the Knights have all disappeared except for that of Bali' Spinola who gave his name to the environs of the fishing harbour of St Julians. Where the old hunting lodges once were there are now the numerous hotels, restaurants and pubs that make St Julian's the most bustling and popular tourist resort in Malta, especially with the younger set.

Left, the Portomaso Tower
in St Julian's, the tallest building
on Malta.

Above and below, two views
of St Julian's.

PACEVILLE - MALTA BY NIGHT

Paceville developed during the 1930s as a district of St Julian's and today is the centre of Malta's nightlife.
The suburb, situated on a hill between Spinola Bay and

Above, St Julian's at night.

Bars and cafés in Paceville.

St George's Bay, is packed with numerous restaurants, discotheques and bars. Paceville also has an elegant Casino. Night owls will find plenty of entertainment here.

The magnificent church of St Lawrence in Vittoriosa. Below, Birgu seen from Senglea. Below, the peninsulas of Birgu and Senglea in Grand Harbour.

Facing page, view of Vittoriosa.

THE THREE CITIES: VITTORIOSA, SENGLEA AND COSPICUA

Collectively known as the Three Cities, the towns by the harbour have, in fact, several names though Vittoriosa, Bormla and Cospicua are those by which they are most commonly known.

Originally *Birgu* (now Vittoriosa) was a small fishing village sheltering behind a castle of unknown antiquity that stood at the very tip of the peninsula. The castle, as the **Castrum Maris**, or **Castell'a Mare**, is mentioned in several medieval documents. Apparently the Castellan had a measure of autonomy and was independent of the Università, the municipal council with its seat in Mdina, and it also appears that the people whose houses were outside the wall of this castle considered themselves as being under the jurisdiction of the Castellan instead of the Università which led to much bad blood between the two authorities. On their arrival in 1530 the Knights decided to settle in

The fine palace on the Xatt-ir-Riżq quay where the Maritime Museum of Birgu is housed.
Left, one of the models displayed in the Museum.

Birgu, in the Fort, as Mdina was too far inland, and immediately set about protecting the hamlet with bastions. Castell'a Mare was strengthened and separated from Birgu by a ditch. Not long afterwards, the adjacent peninsula, then uninhabited and known as *l'Isla* was likewise protected by bastions and by the time Claude de la Sengle was Grand Master it was sufficiently inhabited to merit the name of "**Città Senglea**" named, of course, after the Grand Master. During the Great Siege of 1565 the inhabitants of Birgu and Senglea showed such outstanding courage that the two towns received the honorific titles of **Città Vittoriosa** (the Victorious City), and **Città Invitta** (the Unconquered City) respectively. The conurbation that linked Birgu and Senglea was named "**Bormla**" and as succes-

sive Grand Masters enclosed all three cities with imposing lines of bastions, the *Margarita* and the *Cottonera Lines*, Bormla received the title of **Città Cospicua** (the Noteworthy). While Valletta was being built, the Knights transferred their seat of government from Birgu to Bormla, but the three cities were still very much the centre of the naval activities of the Order; the shipyards and the arsenals were here and consequently the Maltese seamen and ship chandlers lived here.
Piracy was a profession of long standing, but with the arrival of the Order, Maltese corsairs achieved respectability by operating under licence from the Grand Master and by being taxed on their booty! Merchants of several nationalities lived in the Three Cities and traded in slaves and other merchandise acquired

by the corsairs and galleys of the Order. The cosmopolitan character of the Three Cities can still be seen: there are more "foreign" Maltese surnames in this part of the Island than in any other. Under the British, the Three Cities were a hive of activity as the Grand Harbour became the home base of the British Mediterranean Fleet, and at the same time several rich Maltese ship owning families settled in Birgu and Senglea. The docks were enlarged and increased in number and the Castell'a Mare, which the Knights had renamed **Fort St Angelo**, now became a shore establishment of the Navy under the name of H.M.S. St Angelo. Being in close proximity to mili-

Above, the church of St Lawrence in Birgu.

Left, the internal courtyard in the Inquisitor's Palace, Vittoriosa.

Below, two works in the National Museum of Ethnography, located inside the Palace.

Below right, a detail of the curved arches in the Palace courtyard.

tary installations, the Three Cities suffered terribly as a result of enemy bombing during World War II, Senglea in particular. The inhabitants were evacuated to the relative safety of the countryside but many a historic building was irreparably damaged or lost. With the granting of Independence and the subsequent closing down of the military base (a tableau in bronze recreates the farewell ceremony), oil tankers and freighters have replaced destroyers and cruisers in the dockyards. Birgu, despite the Blitz, still has a lot to offer the visitor, such as a number of 16th-century houses in which the Knights made their abode on arrival: the **Inquisitor's Palace**, the magnificent **Church of St. Lawrence** and the **Maritime Museum.** Built in 1660, the *Inquisitor's Palace* is one of the very few remaining examples in Europe of this particular architectural style and probably has survived due to the fact that throughout its five centuries of history it always hosted high-ranking officials. The palace is an architectural masterpiece and now houses the **Museum of Ethnography**. The *Church of St Lawrence* was built over an older medieval church. It was destroyed by a fire but completely rebuilt in 1681 by Lorenzo Gafà. The two towers are later additions, however: the one on the left dates from the 18th century, while the other is 20th century. Exhibited in the *Maritime Museum* are models of ships, paintings, nautical instruments and arms illustrating Malta's seafaring history. Two rooms are also dedicated to the history of the navy of the Knights of Saint John and the British navy. For the energetic, a walk around the **bastions of Senglea** with a camera can be rewarding.

View over Senglea.

Two look-out towers on the ramparts of Senglea.

A view and a monument dedicated to the Immaculate Conception at Cospicua.

VITTORIOSA
AND THE GREAT SIEGE

In 1565 the Turks besieged
Malta with a mighty army. The
troops of the Knights were
greatly inferior numerically and
were garrisoned mainly in the
fortified cities of Vittoriosa and
Senglea. Despite all forecasts
to the contrary, the siege
stretched on for a long time.
Birgu played an important role
as an example of resistance
against the enemy and in
providing aid for the other
cities. Vittoriosa and all the
other major Maltese cities
were attacked repeatedly;
in the end they nevertheless
succeeded in defeating the
Turks, who withdrew on 8th
September. Since then, the
date has been celebrated
as "**Victory Day**" with
a regatta held in Grand
Harbour and contested
by crews from the six
towns on the cove.

PAOLA AND THE ĦAL SAFLIENI HYPOGEUM

Located in the part of Grand Harbour furthest inland, Paola is named after the Grand Master Antoine de Paule who founded it in 1626. The city is most famous for the **Ħal Saflieni Hypogeum** created from 4100 to 2500 B.C. and discovered in 1902 by a group of labourers who were building a house. The Hypogeum consists of three levels, though only the first two can be visited. The structure was used both as a burial place (the remains of about 7000 people have been found here) and as a temple where probably fertility rites took place as the characteristics of the numerous statues found here would seem to indicate (the figure, for example, of the *"Sleeping Woman"* housed in the

Above, the church of Christ the King in Paola, where the Hypogeum is.

Above, the entrance to the Hypogeum of Ħal Saflieni.

National Archaeological Museum of Valletta). The **Chamber of the Oracle** is particularly interesting: the roof is decorated with a tree motif representing the Tree of Life and a small niche amplifies the voice, also creating an echo. It was probably from here that the priests enunciated their oracles.

55

The archaeological site of Tarxien.

TARXIEN TEMPLES

In no other site in Malta is the evolution of prehistoric temple building better exemplified than it is at the **megalithic temples of Tarxien**. The earliest temple, now unfortunately in a vestigial state, goes back to around 2200 B.C., while the more recent of the four temples appeared in a burst of splendour some four hundred years later. The *spiral*, as a decorative motif, is found in many places in Europe from the North Atlantic seaboard to the Aegean; the ones at Tarxien, however,

might have been invented, or at least developed, independently. What was probably the most colossal **stone sculpture** then in existence has been found inside the temples: originally 2.50 metres in height, the statue, presumably representing a *Mother Goddess*, has been broken in half and the top part is missing. There is a lot of conjecture about the significance of the statues of the "Fat Ladies" found in most of the Maltese temples; it is possible that they are examples of female fertility deities prevalent throughout the lands bordering the Mediterranean.

MARSAXLOKK

Marsaxlokk, the harbour to the south-east, is now a small but picturesque harbour where the brightly coloured fishing boats ride at anchor and where the wives of the fishermen knot nylon string bags for the tourists.

But Marsaxlokk is also a microcosm of the historical past of the Island. A short distance from this village is the **archaeological site of Tas-Silġ** still in the process of being excavated; the remains of Late Neolithic megalithic buildings have been found here, greatly modified by superimposed Punic and Byzantine structures; here too are the only remains of a mosque to be found on the island. Norman coins have also been found at Tas-Silġ. To prevent the landing of corsairs in the harbour, the Fort St Lucian was erected at its entrance by the Order. Used as a munitions depot during World War II, it now houses the Marine Research Centre. Marsaxlokk Bay, of which the fishing harbour of Marsaxlokk forms part, is now being converted into a port for container ships.

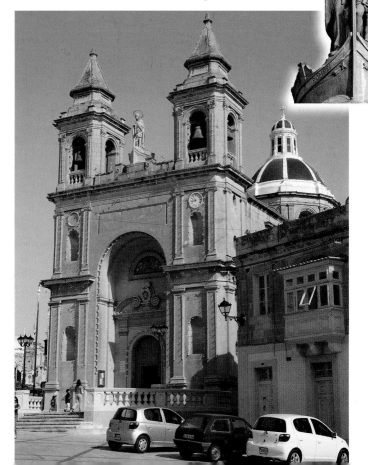

Above, view of the port of Marsaxlokk
with the 'luzzu', characteristic
fishermen's boats.
Right, some souvenirs of Malta.
Below, the Sunday market
at Marsaxlokk: as well as fish
and other foodstuffs, attractive
souvenirs of the archipelago
are sold here.

Opposite page, the church
of Our Lady of Pompei, Marsaxlokk
and a detail of the statue
above the façade.

CHARACTERISTIC MALTESE BOATS

These brightly-colored boats, which derive from Phoenician vessels, are one of the symbols of Malta. The **luzzu** is the traditional fishermen's boat; the **dghajsa** is similar to

the Venetian gondola, but more colourful: it was used to transport both passengers and goods. Today the dghajsa can be seen only in Grand Harbour. The bow of these vessels is decorated with the so-called **"eyes of Osiris,"** a symbol of Phoenician origin that offers protection from all the dangers of the sea.

The Għar Dalam cave where numerous animal fossils have been found.

Left, a skeleton exhibited in the Għar Dalam Museum.

GĦAR DALAM

In the era when the Maltese islands were an extension of the Italian mainland, animals like elephants, hippos, deer and foxes roamed the land. With the rising of the sea-level, or the sinking of the land, or both, the islands were separated from the land mass and these animals were marooned. This took place in the Quaternary Era, some 10,000 years ago, and not during the Pliocene, five million to one million years ago, as was once thought to have been the case.

In time these stranded animals gradually evolved into an island sub-race resulting in a degeneration in some of the species.

Fossil bones of animals have been discovered in caves and fissures in various parts of the island, but the largest concentration to be discovered so far is that at Għar Dalam.

In 1917 **two human molars** were found in this cave and, at the time of their discovery were believed to be those of Neanderthal Man.

However, these molars have now been assigned to a much later period and it can be assumed that when the animals died, and their bones were carried into Għar Dalam by the action of flowing water, man had not yet arrived in Malta. Stone Age man did use Għar Dalam as his abode around 4000 B.C. but by this time these animals had become extinct in the Maltese Islands.

WIED IŻ-ŻURRIEQ, THE BLUE GROTTO AND THE DINGLI CLIFFS

The western coast of Malta is steep and precipitous but in places clefts in the cliffs slope down to sea-level. One such cleft is **Wied iż-Żurrieq**. Looking like a miniature fjord, this narrow arm of the sea provides anchorage for boats in calm weather; at the first sign of a storm the boats are winched up a steep slipway and landed.

The boats at Wied iż-Żurrieq were, and still are, used for fishing; now, however, the fishermen are discovering that it is more lucrative to take visitors to the nearby **Blue Grotto**.

The presence of this deep sea-

Above, the Blue Grotto.
Below, tourists on their way to visit this famous grotto.

Top and left, two views
of the Dingli Cliffs.
Above and right, more views
of the Blue Grotto.

cave, in which the depths are of an unbelievably intense blue, has long been known to the fisher folk. During World War II, when an air-raid alarm was sounded the people here took to their boats and rowed into the cave for safety.

North of the Blue Grotto are the magnificent **Dingli Cliffs**. Stretching for some 5 km, the cliffs rise to 250 m above sea level. At some points the cliffs jut out directly into the sea though at others they form small plains that are often cultivated. The cliffs provide a wonderful panorama.

ĦAĠAR QIM

This Copper Age **temple** was originally built about 2700 B.C. but even then it underwent several modifications.
For some unknown reason the axis of the first structure was altered and the temple itself was several times extended.
The kind of stone used in the building of this temple (Globigerina Limestone) is rather soft and relatively simple to work; possibly for this reason

Views of the Ħaġar Qim temple.

there are several "porthole" openings in Ħaġar Qim.

A **monolith** on the outside of the temple wall has been tentatively interpreted as evidence of phallic worship.

A **pillar "altar"** with an unusual palm frond decorative carving has been found in this temple, but not in any other; it is possible that this pillar was not originally part of the temple furniture and was placed there at a later date.

MNAJDRA

Perhaps having learned that Globigerina Limestone does not resist bad weather, the builders of Mnajdra constructed this temple out of the harder Coralline Limestone which, however, was difficult to work, while the interior walls were faced with a softer kind of limestone.

The best preserved of the **three Mnajdra temples** is interesting for the *secret chambers* that are hidden inside the thickness of its walls; these chambers communicate with the temple proper by holes bored through the wall; it is surmised that statues of gods or goddesses could have been placed in front of these holes and the "priest" hiding in the oracle chamber was the voice of the deity as this "spoke" to the faithful. A healing cult may well have been practised in this temple as a number of baked-clay models of parts of the human body, showing symptoms of disease, have been found here.

The megalithic complex of Mnajdra.

View of Mdina, the old capital of Malta.

MDINA

The Arabs divided the Roman town of Melita in two parts: the citadel they named Mdina (the Town) and the rest of the old settlement they named Rabat (the Suburb), names by which they are still known.

During the medieval period Mdina was the seat of the Municipal government and administrative centre as well as a mustering station for the militia at the approach of the enemy.

At this time too, a number of religious orders built their monasteries outside the walls of Mdina and established themselves at Rabat and its surroundings.

When the Order of the Knights arrived in 1530, they realized they would be better served if they established themselves by the harbour where their galleys lay at anchor, and as a result of this decision they left Mdina and its inhabitants undisturbed.

When Valletta was built and eventually became the capital of the Maltese Islands in 1571, Mdina was relegated to being the *Città Vecchia* (the Old City). Some of the inhabitants of Mdina did migrate to the new city but among those who stayed on were the aristocratic families of Malta who still occupied their ancestral homes there; this had the fortunate effect of preserving a number of old 14th and 15th century houses and palaces. The old Maltese aristocratic families owned large rural properties and from time immemorial the farmers came to Mdina to pay their yearly dues to these nobles on the traditional date of the *Mnarja* (an ancient harvest festival, Christianized into the feast of Saints Peter and Paul).

This feast was, and still is, celebrated under the trees of Malta's nearest thing to a forest, the **Buskett**. Here, in 1586, the Grand

Masters built a hunting lodge and summer retreat known as **Verdala Castle**. Because Roman law forbade burials inside the city, the **catacombs** were located outside the walls of Melita and here too, according to tradition, is the cave in which St Paul was kept prisoner for three months. The **Main Gate** to the City was erected in 1724 by Grand Master De Vilhena, replacing an earlier *drawbridge gate* the outline of which, now walled up, is still visible some metres away to the right of the present gate. It is reached by a narrow *stone bridge*, over a moat dug out by the Arabs, and is decorated with stone trophies of arms supported by lions - the lion forms part of Grand Master Vilhena's escutcheon. On the outside are a *Latin inscription* giving the date and some details of the building of the new gate as well as a *trophy* beautifully carved in stone and decorated with mar-

Above, Mdina's main gate.
Left, a typical medieval house.
Below left, detail of a palace
in the centre of Mdina.
Below, a souvenir shop.

View of the city.

tial and triumphal symbols and with the Grand Master's arms on white marble, surrounded by the *coat-of-arms of the city of Mdina* and those of Vilhena once more. On the inside are the coats of arms of Antonio Inguanez and a Latin inscription which commemorates his action to quell a rebellion in 1428. *Bas-relief carvings of stone* recall the patron saints of the city: St Paul, St Publius and St Agatha. A *headless* *Roman marble statue*, now in the Museum of Roman Antiquities, was once encased in the wall of the main entrance.

There are many beautiful buildings and monuments in this small city, including in particular the 18th century **Vilhena Palace,** now housing the **Museum of Natural History** and the elegant **palaces of Villegaignon Street**, as well as of course, the impressive and austere **Cathedral**.

The elegant façade of St Paul's cathedral.
Below, one of the two towers that frame the façade.

ST PAUL'S CATHEDRAL

According to tradition Malta's earliest Cathedral was dedicated to the Blessed Virgin, Mother of God; dismantled in the Muslim period it was reconstructed and rededicated to St Paul after the Norman conquest.

This old church was modified and enlarged several times. In 1419 a horizontal rectangular wing was added to the edifice; in 1626 Bishop Baldassarre Cagliares added a recess at the back and in 1679 Bishop Molina laid the first stone of the choir which was inaugurated on 28th June 1682.

The terrible earthquake of 11 January 1693 destroyed the old Cathedral almost completely except for the sacristy and the newly constructed choir. The latter

Details of the cathedral interior:
the organ, the high altar, a side chapel
and the vaults of the central nave
with frescoes illustrating the life
of St Paul.

had already been decorated with a fine **altarpiece**, a **painting** representing *St Paul's Conversion* and a **fresco** depicting *St Paul's Shipwreck* as well as *five other works*, all painted by Mattia Preti (1613-1699). These fortunately survived the earthquake.

Building of a larger Cathedral in the new baroque style was immediately taken in hand and entrusted to the Maltese architect Lorenzo Gafà who eleven years before had constructed the apsed choir. There was no need for a new plan: Gafà had previously submitted the plan and wooden model for a church in the new baroque style and the Cathedral Chapter had examined and approved them on 18th May 1692, that is eight months before the earthquake had taken place.

The new Cathedral was completed and consecrated in October 1702 by Bishop Cocco Palmieri (1684-1713) whose coat-of-arms, along with those of the reigning Grand Master Fra Ramon Perellos (1697-1720) and of the City of Mdina, was placed on the façade over the main entrance.

Detail of the baroque entrance to Mdina's Cathedral Museum.

The palace of the Seminary where the Cathedral Museum is located.

CATHEDRAL MUSEUM

The **Cathedral Museum** in Archbishop Square is an imposing baroque palace housing fine **collections of art and archaeology** as well as important archives.

The building, completed in 1744, was constructed as a Diocesan Seminary and served its purpose up to the first decade of the present century; it was then utilized by various ecclesiastical and educational institutions until on 5th January 1969 it was inaugurated by Sir Maurice Dorman, Governor-General of Malta, as the Cathedral's Museum. The main bulk of the art collections results from a **legacy by Count Saverio Marchese** (1757-1833). A newly opened large room on the right of the entrance serves for the temporary display of new acquisitions but the room is also offered to local artists for exhibiting their latest works and for hosting one-man exhibitions.

Above, a painting of the Umbrian school portraying "Saint Catherine of Siena".

Right, the "St Paul polyptych", a masterpiece in the Museum picture gallery. It was an altar panel in the old Cathedral until 1682, subsequently replaced with a painting by Mattia Preti.

Below, one of the works exhibited in the Museum.

MUSIC AND FOLKLORE

On Malta you will have the opportunity to listen to much music linked to local folklore. Every town has one band: this genre is very widespread and is one of the main attractions at the summer festivals and the celebrations dedicated to the local patron saints. The Etnika group, which proposes Maltese ethnic music played with period instruments (trumpets, percussion instruments, and bagpipes) and in a modern key, has also met with great success. There is also the prestigious **Malta Jazz Festival**, held every year on the bastions of Valletta, featuring guests of international fame.

RABAT

Both Rabat and Mdina are perched on a ridge dominating the whole expanse of the island and of the sea beyond. Both centres have been inhabited for thousands of years.

Rabat incorporates a good part of the old Roman city which was reduced to its present dimensions by the Arabs.

This explains how the sumptuous townhouse with its fine polychrome mosaic pavements once inside the Roman town of Melita now forms part of Rabat as the Museum of Roman Antiquities. In the Roman era the Melita area was enriched with palaces and temples, relics of which, such as inscriptions, columns, capitals and mosaics, are now in the *Museum of Roman Antiquities*.

The Rabat area is intimately connected with the introduction of Christianity to the islands: in 60 A.D. St Paul the Apostle, under arrest on his way to Rome and shipwrecked on the island, is said to have lived for three months in a cave within the ditch below the walls of the old Roman city - *St Paul's Grotto* – which he used as a centre for his activity in establishing a primitive Christian community.

Since then the area has been dedicated to St Paul and is overlooked by a church where an important cemetery was located in medieval

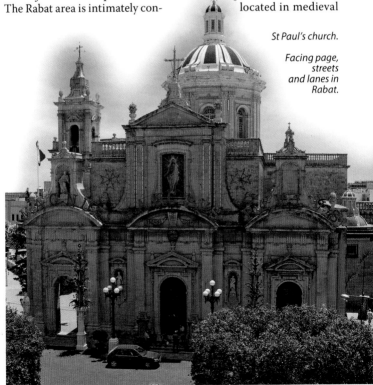

St Paul's church.

Facing page, streets and lanes in Rabat.

A detail of St Paul's church: the upper section of the façade and the dome. Right, the inside of the dome.

times. Burial being prohibited inside the walls of the city, the area outside the ditch, from St Paul's Grotto to Buskett, abounds with a concentration of hypogea - or burial places - of pagan, Jewish or Christian origin dug into the rock by the Phoenicians, Greeks, Romans and Byzantines. Their tombs contain a rich variety of architectural elements. The largest of these are the **St Paul** and the **St Agatha complexes** in the Hal-Bajjada district.

Before the coming of the Knights, Rabat became the centre of various religious orders which preferred to build their houses in a place not far from the capital city but at the same time sufficiently secluded for their monastic retreat. The Knights, concentrated in Vittoriosa and Valletta, erected very

*Some statues in St Paul's church.
Right, the high altar.*

few buildings in Rabat and did little to embellish the area.
Today, besides schools and colleges, Rabat has various social and musical band clubs, a market which is very popular on Sunday mornings, and playing fields. The Rabat area is ideal for walks in the countryside.

ST PAUL'S CHURCH

The main square of Rabat is dominated by the **Church of St Paul**. It stands on the site of the house of the Roman governor, Publius, who was converted to Christianity by St Paul. The present church was designed by Francesco Buonamici, the architect who brought the Baroque style to Malta, and was built by Lorenzo Gafà between 1656 and 1681. The church is particularly noted for its unusual *façade* with three portals. Inside are many works of art portraying scenes from the *life of St Paul*. Near the main entrance is a stairway leading to *St Paul's Grotto*, once the destination of frequent pilgrimages.

Top, St Paul's grotto.
Above the statue of the saint.
Right, an inscription inside the grotto.

ST. PAUL'S GROTTO

This is located in the heart of Rabat next to St Paul's Church. St Paul is reputed to have sheltered here whilst in Malta, and stone from the cave was accorded miraculous powers.

Above, the entrance to the catacombs of St Paul and St Agatha.
Above and right, some passages in the catacombs.

ST. PAUL'S AND ST. AGATHA'S CATACOMBS

These catacombs are well worth a visit, and in summertime offer cool respite from the sun. There are *pagan, Jewish* and *Christian catacombs* with a wide variety of tomb types among the maze of passageways. Note particularly the agape tables or triclinia; round tables hewn out of the rock where commemorative feasts were thought to be held on the anniversaries of deaths.

MUSEUM OF ROMAN ANTIQUITIES

The misnamed **"Roman Villa" Museum** covers the site of a rich and sumptuously decorated town house belonging to a wealthy person in Roman Malta. The site, discovered in 1881 and further excavated in 1920-1924, contains a number of remarkably fine **mosaic polychrome pavements** and some original architectural elements. A number of rooms were constructed to protect the mosaics and an upper hall was added to provide exhibition space and a suitable entrance. The porticoed neo-classical **façade** was completed in 1925.

Above, vases exhibited in the Museum.

Below, statues and Roman columns displayed in the Museum.

The neo-classical façade of the Museum of Roman Antiquities.

Right, wonderful mosaic pavements.

Below, a detail of the mosaics.

85

MOSTA

*Mosta is roughly in the geographical centre
of the Island of Malta and, in times gone by,
it was considered to be far enough inland to be
relatively safe from corsair attacks.*

Typical balconies in the streets of Mosta.

*Facing page, above, the church.
Below, the interior of the majestic dome and the high altar.*

Given its position, Mosta is an important crossroads lying on the route for those travelling from the south and the east towards the north of the island. The chief attraction is now the monumental church, dedicated to the Assumption and called **St Mary's**, with its circular design which was inspired by the Pantheon in Rome. Its *dome* is the third largest in Europe, the two other domes being in Rome and in London. The building was started in 1833 and the church was consecrated in 1871; it was built around and over an earlier church which continued to be used during the period when work was in progress. In today's machine age it might seem that construction took an exceedingly long time, but it should be remembered that work on the church was done on a voluntary basis, in the little spare time that the labourers had at their disposal. Like many other of the old churches in Malta therefore, this is a true monument of faith.

In 1942 a thousand pound bomb penetrated St Mary's, piercing the dome and rolling through the interior but without exploding.

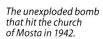

The unexploded bomb that hit the church of Mosta in 1942.

BUĠIBBA

Until just a few years ago Buġibba and its extension **Qawra** were a rocky and barren headland with no particular point of interest; at its tip is a small coastal garrison of the Order which surrounds an older watchtower. Further inland is a small **prehistoric temple**, in a poor state of preservation, but rather unique as it was decorated with carvings of fish (these bas-reliefs are now preserved in the National Museum of Archeology in Valletta). Buġibba and Qawra now form one of the most popular summer resorts in the north of the Island, filled with the noise and bustle that some holiday-makers enjoy and consider "rest". The tower and garrison at the tip of Qawra has now been turned into a restaurant while the prehistoric temple is preserved in situ within the precincts of a hotel.

Below, a view of Qawra.

Above, a view of splendid Buġibba.

ST. PAUL'S BAY

St. Paul's Bay is one of the older sea-side resorts. At the turn of the century it was the fashion for persons of means to have a second home on the coast in which to pass the hot summer months in peace and quiet, but also in comfort. St. Paul's is now a residential area and an aura of tranquility still pervades the place.

The town of San Pawl il-Baħar (more accurately translated as St. Paul by-the-sea, rather than St. Paul's Bay) has many reminders of its namesake – one of Christ's Apostles. Here one can see **Ghajn Rażul**, the Apostle's Fount, at which the saint is reputed to have quenched his thirst following his shipwreck; the **church at tal-Ħuġġieġa**, the church of the bonfire, marking the site where the apostle cast the viper into the flames and the **church at San Pawl Milqgħi**, the place where St. Paul was welcomed by Publius, the Roman Governor. A number of churches have been built successively on this last site and, significantly, at the lowest level of the archaeological site, Roman remains have come to light.

*Popeye's Village in Anchor Bay.
Below, Golden Bay.*

THE NORTH: THE LOVELIEST BAYS AND BEACHES OF MALTA

Continuing to the north we reach the town of **Mellieħa**, overlooking the bay of Mellieħa.

The longest stretch of sand in all of Malta is here and the calm waters of the bay make it an ideal beach for families. Not far from Mellieħa, but on the west coast, is **Anchor Bay** where the clear waters are full of fish making it a perfect spot

Golden Bay with a lookout tower dating from 1637 in the background. Below left, Għajn Tuffieħa Bay and Ġnejna Bay.

for divers. Robert Altman made his film *Popeye* in this bay. Also on the west coast are the most enchanting and famous bays of Malta: **Golden Bay**, which is the best equipped beach of the island, **Għajn Tuffieħa Bay** and **Ġnejna Bay**. These are some of the finest beaches on the island and lovers of the sea will certainly appreciate their beauty.

COMINO

*The little island of Comino is named
after a plant that grows on its shingly earth:
wild fennel or cumin.*

For long periods of its history Comino was an unsafe place in which to live, nevertheless, people did inhabit this tiny island on and off, and the population figures fluctuate from nil to sparse.

In 1416 the Maltese petitioned the Aragonese king, Alphonse V, to build a tower on Comino as a deterrent to the corsairs

who made it their base, but the people of the island had to wait two hundred years before work was taken in hand; eventually the **Tower** of Comino was finished under Grand Master Alof de Wignacourt in 1618.

Despite the protection of the tower, people were wary of making Comino their home and the ancient church here was, in fact, deconsecrated in 1667 as being derelict; in 1716 the church was repaired and reconsecrated and by this time the island had been repopulated to some extent.

With its handful of resident families and a single hotel, Comino, even now, has an air of a forsaken but beautiful island.

THE BLUE LAGOON

The principal attraction of Comino is the marvellous Blue Lagoon on the west coast of the island. The crystalline waters lapping the sparkling white sand beach are perfect for a swim and for snorkeling.

Right, the splendid Blue Lagoon. Below, Comino and the little island of Cominotto.

Facing page, the tower built by Wignacourt.

EXPLORING THE DEPTHS!

The Maltese archipelago, with its three principal islands (Malta, the largest; Comino, famous for its Blue Lagoon; and Gozo, the island of Calypso), is the ideal spot for underwater sports. The waters of Malta's sea are among the most transparent and uncontaminated in the entire Mediterranean; the temperature varies between 23° C in the summer and 13°-15° C in winter. Diving in these waters is a unique and unforgettable experience among an exuberance of brightly-colored marine flora and fauna. Many different species of fish are there for the seeing: sea bass, mullets, flying-fish, and the extremely rare Golden Perch, which risks extinction in the Mediterranean. But fish-watching is not an activity

limited solely to summer: even in
the winter the visitor will marvel
at such magnificent examples
as St. Peter's fish, which swims
close to shore. Both beginners
and experienced divers will
find many opportunities for
underwater adventure in Malta
and the chance to discover and
explore natural ports, solitary
bays, sheltered inlets, rocky
cliffs, and even shipwrecks.

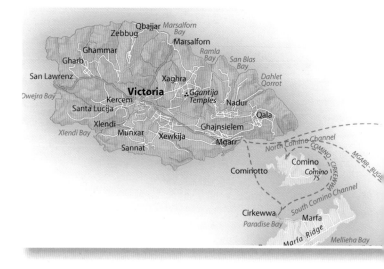

The port of Mġarr on the island of Gozo.

Opposite page, a cruise ship.

GOZO

Some years ago it was planned to connect the islands of Malta and Gozo by a bridge and Japanese engineers were called in to carry out a feasibility study.

The project was considered technically possible but as the expense involved would have been considerable the plan was shelved. And many people in Malta, and many more in Gozo breathed a sigh of relief. Should the Island of Gozo become too accessible there is a real danger of the island losing the old-world charm which Gozo has so far retained, and which Malta once possessed but unfortunately began to loose some half century ago. Malta's smaller sister island is different in that it is more fertile, more picturesque, and far more unspoilt; but what makes Gozo so markedly different from Malta are the Gozitans.

These frugal and tough people seem to be proof against

A view of Mġarr, Gozo's port, showing the church of Our Lady of Lourdes. Opposite, the brightly coloured luzzu fishing boats.

any adversity; their character is tempered by privations and constant danger and, as a result of their frequent ordeals, they and their descendants have emerged strong and resilient. Malta and Gozo share the same history and historical remains are duplicated in the two islands, but Gozo has had more than its share of misfortunes. Largely undefended, the island has many times been devastated by pirate attacks and on one occasion almost the whole of the population was carried into slavery. When Gozitans had advance warning of an impending invasion, such as the Great Siege, some of them sought refuge in the better fortified towns of Malta and some of the elderly were evacuated to Sicily, but they always returned home as soon as it was safe for them to do so. Gozitans ransomed from slavery also returned home, never decid-

ing or desiring to settle in a safer place; Gozitan emigrants who become wealthy in the countries of their adoption likewise return home and build grand houses for themselves as evidence of their success. Perhaps what makes Gozo special is the love and quiet pride of its inhabitants for their homeland. This pride is reflected, among other things, in the size and beauty of their churches.

Aerial view of the Citadel.

VICTORIA

The Gozitans always use the name of Rabat; it is the only town in Gozo and was named Victoria in 1897.

It is in the centre of the island and has been the capital of Gozo probably from Roman times. Nothing structurally very old has survived but in the haphazard, twisting lanes and alley-ways of the town, splendid balconies and grand palaces revealing features of local architecture are still to be seen.

THE CITADEL

The Citadel is built on one of the many flat-topped hills in the centre of Gozo. Its origins can be traced to the late Middle Ages. At one time the entire population of Gozo was obliged to take shelter within these walls after sunset. The **walls** themselves date back from the 16th to the 18th century. Most of the buildings inside the Citadel are in ruins but the **Old Courts of Law** and the **Old Governor's Palace** are still being used as the Law Courts of Gozo. There are also the **Old Prisons** and the **Armoury of the Knights**, the *Archaeological, Natural History* and *Folklore Museums*.

The **Cathedral**, together with the **Bishop's Palace** and the **Cathedral Museum**, dominates the Citadel.

The Citadel.
Above, the bell
tower of St Mary's
Cathedral and a view
of the walls.

Right, the clock
near the island's port.

Below, narrow lanes
and buildings
in the Citadel.

Following page,
the façade of St
Mary's Cathedral
and a view
of the church.

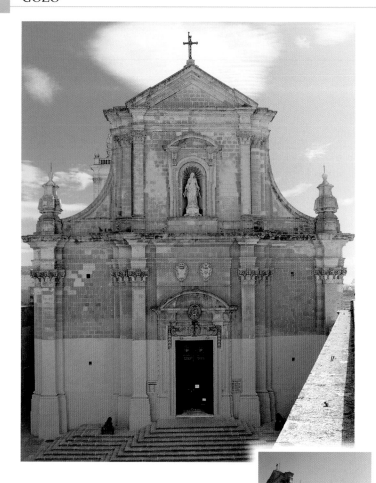

THE CATHEDRAL

The Cathedral designed by the Maltese architect Lorenzo Gafà in the form of a Latin cross was built between 1697 and 1711 on the site of an older church. Inside, one's attention is drawn instantly to the flat trompe l'oeil *ceiling* depicting the interior of a dome painted by Antonio Manuele of Messina in 1739. There are paintings by the Maltese Giuseppe Hyzler, Michele Busuttil and Tommaso Madiona. Also of interest are the *high altar* inlaid with precious malachite and the *baptismal font* and its replica on either side of the main door sculpted from blocks of Gozo onyx.

The interior of the Cathedral: the dome, the high altar and the central nave.

*Above, an interior, an old millstone for grain,
and the entrance to the Ethnographic Museum.*

FOLKLORE MUSEUM

This Museum is located in three late medieval houses with Sicilian-influenced architectural features. Exhibits consist of *agricultural implements* which include a *mill for grinding corn*, *items* related to the cotton industry, *tools* used in different crafts and some traditional costumes.

A room in the Museum.

ARCHAEOLOGICAL MUSEUM

All archaeological material found in Gozo is now exhibited in this 17th-century house known as *Casa Bondi*. Of special interest are **shards of the Għar Dalam period** (5000 B.C.) found at Għajn Abdul, probably the oldest ever found in the Maltese islands, and the **Majmuna tombstone**, a beautiful marble inscription in Kufic characters dating to 1174 A.D.

Some archaeological items exhibited in the Museum: amphora, coins and the burial stone of Majmuna.

View of Victoria and St George's church.
Right, detail of the church.

ST. GEORGE'S CHURCH

St George's Parish covers almost half of Victoria. This church was built in the 1670's and suffered severe damage in the earthquake of 1693. A new façade was built in 1818. The dome and the aisles are of recent construction. There are many works of art in this church which include the *paintings of the dome* and *ceiling* by Gian Battista Conti of Rome and other paintings by Giuseppe Cali, Stefano Erardi and Mattia Preti.

The area over which the church is built is of considerable archaeological interest dating at least to the Roman period.

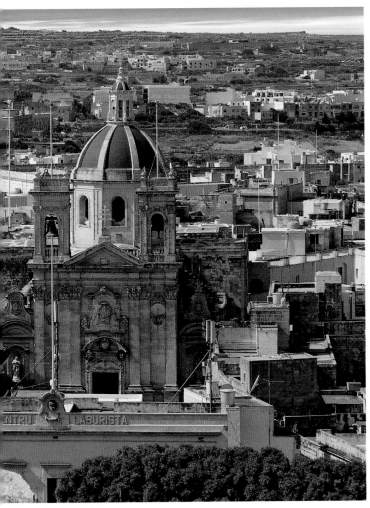

Some views of the market and the shops of It-Tokk.

IT-TOKK

The area has probably always been the centre and the market place of Victoria and still is to-day: in the morning It-Tokk is bristling with activity. In the side streets round the square one can buy the delicious Gozo nougat, the "*bankuncini*" (almond based cakes) and the "*pasti tas-salib*" which are Gozo's sweet specialities.

Two views of the old fishing village of Xlendi.

XLENDI

This is another summer resort used by the locals and tourists alike. In 1961 two shipwrecks dating to about the 2nd century B.C. and 5th A.D. were located on the sea-bed at the mouth of Xlendi Creek under 35 metres of water. Many amphorae and several lead anchor stocks have been recovered from these wrecks and are now at the **Gozo Museum of Archaeology.**

DWEJRA

Dwejra is an area of outstanding natural beauty on the north-western coast of Gozo. It has been an attraction to the visitor for many centuries and representations of the Fungus Rock are to be found in many old engravings.

The area in itself is a veritable museum of history, archaeology, natural history and geology.

INLAND SEA

The Gozitans call it *"Il-Qawra"*. This sea-filled basin is surrounded partly by the high cliffs and partly by a pebbly beach. The sea enters through a natural tunnel in the cliffs creating a vast **pool** of clear sea water. The sea here is warmer and is excellent for bathing, especially for children. It gets deeper as one nears the tunnel.

Diving enthusiasts at Dwejra. Below, the Inland Sea.

"Fungus Rock" also known locally as the "General's Rock".

FUNGUS ROCK

The locals call it "**il-Ġebla tal-Ġeneral**" (the General's Rock) as it is said that a Commander of the Order of St John discovered a **shrub** here which is known locally as *"Gherq Sinjur"* (*Cynomorium coccineum Linn*). The plant was jealously protected by the Knights of St John as it was believed to possess great medicinal properties against certain ailments and illnesses. In 1744 Grandmaster Pinto rendered the rock completely inaccessible from all directions. The rock was also guarded from the mainland and until the middle of the last century the Government employed a guardian for Fungus Rock.

The "Zerka Window", the impressive natural arch rising out of the sea.

THE ZERKA WINDOW

This is a massive natural archway rising out of the sea. Though it is also called **It-Tieqa** (the window) by the locals, it looks more like a door. The sea around it is intensely blue and provides some of the finest snorkel swimming in Malta and Gozo. There is an **underwater cave** close by, known as "**Il-Hofra tal-Bedwin**" (the peasant's hole) which is of exceptional beauty. One can take a trip in one of the small fishing boats of the Inland Sea round the Zerka Window and the Fungus Rock.

111

Ta' Pinu Sanctuary.

TA' PINU SANCTUARY

This is a national shrine and a centre of pilgrimage for both the Gozitans and the Maltese. On this spot there was a 16th century **chapel** dedicated to Our Lady of the Assumption with an *altarpiece* painted by Amedeo Perugino in 1619.

On June 22nd 1883, Carmela Grima a middle aged peasant woman is reported to have heard the voice of Our Lady speak to her here and this was followed by numerous acts of grace and miracles of healing while Gozo also succeeded in avoiding the plague the following year. Offerings were sent to this chapel from all over the Maltese Islands as well as from abroad.

The present church was begun in 1920 and was consecrated in 1931. It was raised to the status of basilica by Pope Pius IX a year later. The old chapel with the original painting can still be seen at the very end of the church where votive offerings are placed on either side of the shrine.

Built in the Romanesque style, this church rises majestically isolated in the unspoilt Gozitan countryside surrounded by the hills of Għammar and Gordan. It is a perfect example of craftsmanship in Maltese stone. Many intricate and different designs are sculpted inside in the same stone, and the mosaic adorning the altarpieces and the friezes in the nave are worthy of note.

A set of life-size Carrara marble *statues* representing the Stations of the Cross have been erected along Għammar Hill overlooking the Ta' Pinu Sanctuary.

ŻEBBUĠ

QBAJJAR SALT-PANS

Like most of the Gozo Churches, the **Church of the Assumption** at Żebbuġ is built in the baroque style. It was consecrated in 1726 and was the first church in Gozo to be built with aisles. Several pieces of beautiful *sculpture* produced from Gozo onyx, like the *high altar*, embellish this church.

From a distance, when filled with sea water, they look not unlike puddles.
The Qbajjar Salt Pans are the biggest salt-works in Gozo. Several tons of sea salt are produced there every year.

The church of the Assumption at Żebbuġ and the canon in front of the entrance.

Two views of the Qbajjar salt marshes.

THE CRAFTS OF MALTA

The Maltese crafts tradition is a long and rich one. One of the best-known products is the **bobbin** or **pillow lace** produced in Gozo and known

for its intricate motifs. This type of hand work was introduced in the 17th century (even though it became well-established only in the 19th), when Genoese lace-makers came to the island. Maltese lace is therefore a variant of that produced in Genoa, even though it has many characteristic features, like inclusion of the Maltese Cross in the patterns. In the streets of Gozo, women still sit outside their homes to work with their pillows, pins, and bobbins, just as they did many years ago. Another important craft is Maltese **silversmithing**, which developed during the era of the Knights and is held in high esteem all over the world even

today. In the jewelry shops you'll find beautiful gold and silver filigree work in ancient and more modern patterns. Malta's production of **vases** and multicoloured **glass** is also highly renowned. The glass is still blown, hand-finished, and finally painted in lively colours.

Fishermen in the port of Marsalforn.
View of Marsalforn and its harbour.

MARSALFORN

This is the most popular summer seaside resort in Gozo.
During summer, especially, the place is crowded with Gozitans and Maltese as well as tourists.
It started as a fishing village and the fishermen still keep their colourful boats in one sheltered corner of the bay.
Fresh fish is found in restaurants here throughout the year. During the hot weather one can indulge in all kinds of aquatic sports.
Bus transport to Victoria is in operation throughout the year at all times of the day and is more frequent during the summer. Marsalforn has a small sandy beach, several hotels, guesthouses, holiday flats, good restaurants, many souvenir shops offering all kinds of Gozitan handicrafts and other tourist amenities.

Round the western headland are the coves of *Qbajjar*, *Xwejni* and the fjord-like cove of *Wied il-Ghasri*.

On the eastern headland are *Ghar Qawqla*, *Ghajn Barrani* and *Ramla Bay*.

More views of this picturesque village and its harbour.

CALYPSO'S CAVE

Calypso's Cave takes one back to the legendary days of Homer. Though it is hard to compare the present state of the cave and its surroundings with Homer's description of Calypso's dwelling place, prehistoric shards of the Ġgantija phase around 3600 B.C. have been found a few metres away from the mouth of the cave. This site has been acclaimed as Calypso's Cave for many years. From the heights of the cave, the view stretches over the valley of Ramla and the red sand dunes of the Bay below.

RAMLA BAY

Ramla is a fine sandy beach on the north coast of Gozo, the best in both islands. Its name means "sandy" and it is an excellent spot for swimming and a wonderful place for children to play.

The brick-red sand of the beautiful beach at Ramla Bay.

XAGHRA

Xaghra became a parish in April 1688 together with Nadur, Sannat and Żebbuġ. The celebration in honour of the patron saint "Our Lady of Victories" is held every year with great pomp on 8th of September.

The **windmill** was built in 1724 together with one at Nadur and another at Għarb, by the Portuguese Grandmaster Manoel de Vilhena. A report drawn up in 1779 by a master mason employed by the Order of St John stated that this windmill was structurally defective. It was suggested that it be pulled down and rebuilt, however this never happened. This mill, like the other at Qala, is currently in a poor state of repair. However, there is hope that it will soon find a suitable guardian and be restored to its original proud appearance together with other places of interest in the village of Xaghra.

Above, the windmill at Xaghra.

The church of Our Lady of Victory.

ĠGANTIJA TEMPLES

The Ġgantija or, as it was commonly known in the past, "*The Giants' Tower*", is the best preserved and by far the most impressive prehistoric temple. It is probably the finest of all the ancient remains in these islands and can compare with Stonehenge for grandeur. It was uncovered about 1826.

Ġgantija consists of two separate systems of courtyards which do not interconnect. They are known as the **South Temple** which is bigger, earlier (c. 3600 B.C.) and better preserved, incorporating five large apses, and the **North Temple** which is smaller and a later addition (c. 3000 B.C.) with a 4-apse structure. The great court of the South Temple measures 23 metres from apse to apse and the height of the wall here is preserved at eight metres, the highest of all the temples. The arch was not yet known in building construction and the span of the apses here is quite large for any conceivable stone roofing. Wood or animal hides might originally have been used as roofing material. Two

kinds of stone were used in the construction; "talfranka", the soft stone mainly used inside as portals and floor slabs, and "tal-qawwi", a harder stone which is mostly used for the general construction of the walls. The interior of the walls was plastered and painted with red ochre. Traces of this have been found. The huge megaliths forming the *outer wall* (the largest weighing several tons) were built alternately, one horizontally and one upright. The space between the inner and outer walls is filled with rubble and earth and it is this system which has given the Ġgantija the necessary stability to withstand the depredations of more than 5000 years. The *floor* is partly covered with soft stone slabs and partly with "torba", or beaten earth. Spiral and pitted designs decorate some of the soft stone slabs. One can hardly see the spirals today but when the site was uncovered they were found in a good state of preservation indicating that the temples had some kind of roofing protection while they were in use.

These pages, the Northern and the Southern Temples at Ġgantija.

121

NINU'S GROTTO

Ninu's Grotto is situated at No. 17 January Str., Xaghra, near the church.

In this Grotto one can see multitudes of stalactites hanging like icicles from the ceiling while many different formations of stalagmites crop up from the floor of the cave.

XEWKIJA

The **church** of Xewkjia is dedicated to St John the Baptist and its dome is one of the largest in the world.

The building was started in 1952 and finished in 1973. It was built round the previous parish church which continued to be used for religious functions until it was pulled down in 1972. The **dome** of Xewkjia was intended to be larger than that of the church of Mosta on Malta. Xewkjia is higher but the diameter is smaller.

There are several good *paintings* in this church. Besides the *altarpiece* by Gioacchino Loretta, a pupil of Mattia Preti, there are three excellent works by Francesco Zahra, the most important Maltese painter of the 18th century. Attached to the Rotunda is the **Church Museum**, where one

The church of St John the Baptist at Xewkija.

*Above, another view
of the Rotunda.
Right, the majestic dome
of the church of St John
the Baptist.
Below, a detail: the statue
of St Zachary.*

can see the treasures and some sculptural works from the old church which was a masterpiece of baroque architecture.

DIMENSIONS

Internal length	63,30 m
Internal width	42,60 m
Internal circumference of dome	25,00 m
Height of church	74,60 m
External circumference	86,00 m
Weight of dome	45,00t

MALTESE CUISINE

Like every other Mediterranean country, Malta is blessed with fresh fish, tasty vegetables, sweet fruit and an abundance of lemons, olives, garlic and capers, mint, basil and much more sun soaked produce enabling the Maltese cook to prepare the most appetising dishes whether traditional or innovative. Maltese dishes generally fall into two categories: peasant cooking with its roots deep in the nation's history and probably little changed over the centuries. This is represented by the thick vegetable soups and stews, oven bakes of uncovered bread (ftira), goats cheeses and potatoes.

Other Maltese dishes have their counterparts throughout the Mediterranean and may be identified with various neighbours: timpana with the Sicilian timballo, and stuffed peppers and aubergines with the Levant. Helwa and imqaret, two favourite sweets, have probably Arabian origins.

If the Maltese table has something to be proud of, it is undoubtedly its bread. The true Maltese hobza is crisp and crunchy on the outside and beautifully light and soft on the inside. Apart from eating it in the usual ways, such as for sandwiches and as an accompaniment

to one's meal or cheese, it is at its best as "Hobz biz-zejt" - literally bread with oil.

MALTESE WINES

It is generally believed that the vine was introduced to Malta by the first Phoenician settlers. Except for the Arab period, viticulture in Malta flourished right up to the arrival of the British. By the end of the 19th century a replanting programme was started and viticulture flourished once again. Sizeable areas of land are now planted with international varieties such as Chardonnay and Merlot.

Like most other Mediterranean countries, Malta has ideal soil and climate conditions to grow excellent wines. Most traditional grape producers still grow local grape varieties (the white variety Ghirgentina and the red variety Gellewza).

GOZO

COMINO

MEDITERRANEAN SEA

N

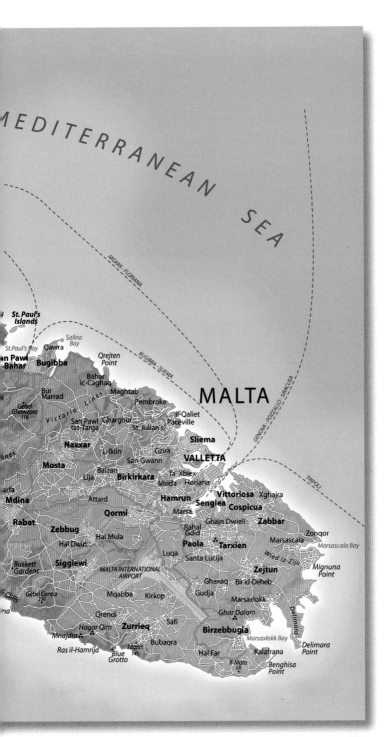

MEDITERRANEAN SEA

MALTA

St. Paul's Islands

St.Paul's Bay
Salina Bay
Qawra
Qrejten Point

an Pawl
Bahar
Bugibba

Bahar ic-Caghaq
Maghtab
Pembroke

Bur Marrad

Gebel Ghawzara 116

San Pawl tat-Targa
Gharghur
St. Julian's
Il-Qaliet
Paceville

Victoria Lines

Naxxar
L-Iklin
San Gwann
Gzira
Sliema

Mosta
Balzan
Lija
Birkirkara
VALLETTA

Ta' Xbiex
Msida
Floriana

arfa

Mdina
Attard
Hamrun
Vittoriosa
Xghajra
Senglea
Cospicua

Rabat
Qormi
Marsa
Ghajn Dwieli
Zabbar

Zebbug
Hal Mula
Rahal Gdid
Paola
Tarxien
Zonqor
Marsascala
Marsascala Bay

Hal Dwin
Luqa
Santa Lucija
Zejtun
Wied iz-Ziju
Mignuna Point

Buskett Gardens
Siggiewi
MALTA INTERNATIONAL AIRPORT
Ghaxaq
Bir id-Deheb

Gebel Ciantar 256
Mqabba
Kirkop
Gudja
Marsaxlokk

Cliffs
Qrendi
Safi
Ghar Dalam

ana
Hagar Qim
Zurrieq
Birzebbugia
Marsaxlokk Bay
Delimara Point

Mnajdra
Bubaqra
Nigret 145
Hal Far
Kalafrana
Benghisa Point
Il-Mara 58

Ras il-Hamrija
Blue Grotto

MGARR - FLORIANA
BUGIBBA - SLIEMA
GENOVA - POZZALLO - SIRACUSA
TRIPOLI

Grand Harbour

127

INDEX

Introduction 3

Prehistory 3
The Phoenicians 4
The Romans 5
Saint Paul 5
The Arabs 6
The Middle Ages 7
The Knights
    of the Order of St John 8
The Great Siege 9
The Foundation of Valletta ... 10
The Fall of the Order 10
The French 10
The British 11
The Path to Independence 12

MALTA 17
VALLETTA 19
- Grand Masters' Palace 22
- Armoury Museum 27
- St John's Co-Cathedral 28
- Republic Street and
    Merchants Street 34
- National Museum
    of Fine Arts 35
- Auberge de Provence
    and the National Museum
    of Archaeology 36
- Auberge de Castille 38
- Barracca Gardens 39
- Fort St Elmo 41
- National War Museum 41
SLIEMA AND ST. JULIAN'S 44
THE THREE CITIES:
    VITTORIOSA, SENGLEA
    AND COSPICUA 49
PAOLA AND THE ḤAL
    SAFLIENI HYPOGEUM 55
TARXIEN TEMPLES 56
MARSAXLOKK 58
GHAR DALAM 62
WIED IŻ-ŻURRIEQ,
    THE BLUE GROTTO AND
    THE DINGLI CLIFFS 63
ḤAĠAR QIM 66
MNAJDRA 68
MDINA 69
- St Paul's Cathedral 72
- Cathedral Museum 75
RABAT 79
- St Paul's Church 81
- St. Paul's Grotto 82
- St. Paul's and St. Agatha's

Catacombs 83
- Museum of Roman
    Antiquities 84
MOSTA 86
BUĠIBBA 88
ST. PAUL'S BAY 89
THE NORTH: THE
    LOVELIEST BAYS AND
    BEACHES OF MALTA 90

COMINO 92

GOZO 97
VICTORIA 100
- The Citadel 100
- The Cathedral 102
- Folklore Museum 104
- Archaeological Museum ... 105
- St. George's Church 106
- It-Tokk 108
XLENDI 109
DWEJRA 110
- Inland Sea 110
FUNGUS ROCK 111
ZERKA WINDOW 111
TA' PINU SANCTUARY 112
ŻEBBUĠ 113
QBAJJAR SALT-PANS 113
MARSALFORN 116
RAMLA BAY 118
XAGHRA 119
ĠGANTIJA TEMPLES 120
XEWKIJA 122

Map 126

CONTEXTS
The Auberges 37
The Blue Lagoon 93
Calypso's Cave 118
Characteristic Maltese Boats... 60
Caravaggio in Malta 33
Carnival 42
The crafts of Malta 114
Exploring the depths! 94
The Maltese Cross 11
Maltese Cuisine 124
Maltese Wines 125
Music and Folklore 76
Ninu's Grotto 122
Paceville – Malta by night 47
Tour of the Grand Harbour .. 43
Vittoriosa
    and the Great Siege 54